Dump Trucks

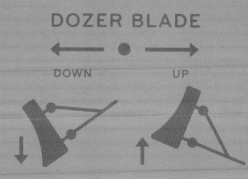

DOZER BLADE

DOWN   UP

Published by Creative Education

P.O. Box 227, Mankato, Minnesota 56002

Creative Education is an imprint of The Creative Company

www.thecreativecompany.us

Design and production by Rob & Damia Design

Art direction by Rita Marshall

Printed in the United States of America

Photographs by Getty Images (Carl Iwasaki//Time & Life Pictures),
iStockphoto (Elena Aliaga, David Dear, David Freund, Robert Hardholt,
Britta Kasholm-Tengve, Shaun Lowe, Jerry McElroy, Pete Muller,
Amy Myers, Maciej Noskowski, Robert Pernell, Jim Pruitt, John Zellmer)

Library of Congress Cataloging-in-Publication Data

Gilbert, Sara.
Dump trucks / by Sara Gilbert.
p. cm. — (Machines that build)
Includes index.
ISBN 978-1-58341-730-0
1. Earthmoving machinery—Juvenile literature. 2. Dump trucks—Juvenile literature.
I. Title. II. Series.

TA725.G53 2009
629.225—dc22   2007051664

First edition
9 8 7 6 5 4 3 2 1

DIESEL FUEL

OFF | | | ON

ENGINE OIL

SEATBELTS

Dump Trucks

sara gilbert
machines that build

A dump truck is a big machine. It can carry almost anything. Dump trucks work at construction (*con-STRUK-shun*) sites for buildings and roads. They help other machines do their jobs.

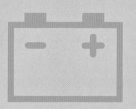

A digger drops dirt into the back of a dump truck.

*Dump trucks take away
extra dirt that is not needed.*

Dump trucks are used to *haul* heavy loads. They carry dirt, rocks, and other things to construction sites. They take *rubble* and trash away. Dump trucks are always on the go!

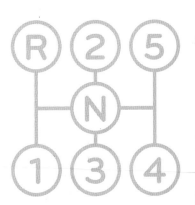

The bed is lifted up to dump the truck's load.

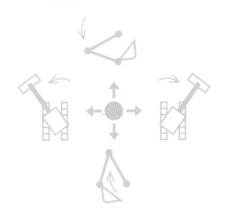

Most dump trucks have a cab in the front. The cab is a place where the *operator* sits to drive the truck. The truck *bed* is behind the cab.

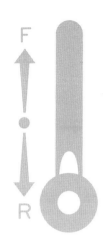

A full-grown elephant

Dump trucks are heavy machines, even when they are empty. Some weigh 80,000 pounds (36 t). Those dump trucks can carry 88,000 pounds (40 t). That is almost as much as six full-grown elephants weigh!

Dump trucks are strong enough to carry heavy loads.

The first dump trucks were built in the early 1900s. They were smaller than dump trucks are today. Some were used as garbage trucks. Other dump trucks helped haul concrete to make roads and *dams*.

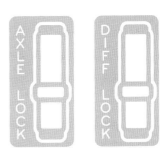

Some dump trucks help build dams by piling up rocks.

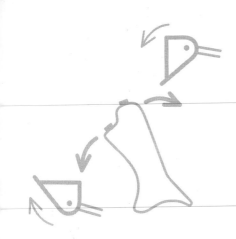

Some dump trucks are short and small so they can work in tight places. Taller trucks can carry bigger loads. Some dump trucks have special jobs, like plowing snow.

Dump trucks can work anywhere and in any weather.

*Very large dump trucks can
be used at mining sites.*

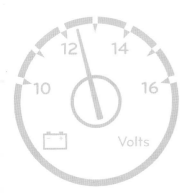

The biggest dump trucks cannot drive on roads. They are hauled to worksites in smaller pieces. Then the pieces are put together to make the trucks. When the work is done, the trucks are taken apart again.

R ← (N) → F

Other big machines called excavators (*EX-kuh-vay-terz*) and backhoes put things in dump trucks. They lift loads of dirt, rocks, or sand into the truck bed. When the bed is full, the dump truck takes the load away.

BACKHOE PATTERN

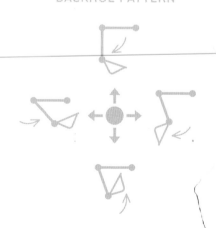

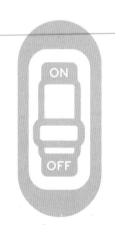

Dump trucks are useful when buildings are torn down.

A dump truck unloads a lot of gravel to make a road.

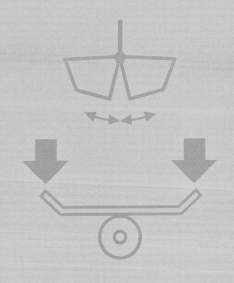

The operator pulls levers and pushes buttons in the cab to dump the load. The bed tips up, and whatever is inside it slides out. Then the bed lowers down. Now the dump truck is ready to pick up another load!

Activity: **Be a Dump Truck**

Find three different boxes of different sizes. Try to choose a narrow box, a wide box, and a flat box (or box lid) with low sides. Fill each one up with blocks, toys, or dirt (be sure to keep it outside). Then tip the boxes on end, and dump out the stuff inside. Which one holds the most? Which one is the easiest to dump out?

Glossary

bed: the back of a dump truck, where things are carried

dams: big walls built to hold back water from a lake or river

haul: to carry a load from one place to another

operator: the person who controls a machine

rubble: broken pieces of stone, brick, and other things used to make buildings

Read More About It

Bridges, Sarah. *I Drive a Dump Truck.* Minneapolis: Picture Window Books, 2004.

Llewellyn, Claire. *Mighty Machines: Truck.* New York: DK Publishing, 2000.

Index